THE
Archive Photographs
SERIES

DARTFORD

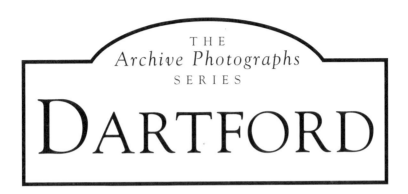

THE Archive Photographs SERIES

DARTFORD

Compiled by
Peter Boreham and Nick Harris

DARTFORD
Borough Council

CHALFORD

First published 1995
Copyright © Peter Boreham and Nick Harris, 1995

The Chalford Publishing Company
St Mary's Mill, Chalford,
Stroud, Gloucestershire, GL6 8NX

ISBN 0 7524 0141 6

Typesetting and origination by
The Chalford Publishing Company
Printed in Great Britain by
Redwood Books, Trowbridge

A Leyland lorry belonging to C.N. Kidd and Sons, brewers of Hythe Street, Dartford. The vehicle is decorated for a special occasion, possibly the annual Gala organised on behalf of the Livingstone Hospital.

Contents

Acknowledgements

The authors would like to thank Chris Baker, Assistant Curator at the Dartford Borough Museum for his help in the compilation of this book.

Thanks are also due to the following individuals who have donated photographs which have been included in the book: Mrs Anderson, Mr Apted, Miss Bird, Mr Brett, Mr Broad, Dr Burne, Mrs Chattenton, Miss Croucher, Miss Curd, Mr Cutten, Mr Davis, Mrs Growns, Mr Gritton, Mr Hall, Mrs Harrison, Mrs Hayden, Mrs Houlston, Mr Hughes, Mrs Jarvis, Mr McKerran, Mrs Maguire, Mr Meakins, Miss Potter, Mr Quinton, Mr Roberts, Mrs Stocker, Miss Terry and Mr Whiting.

Introduction

While the human history of Dartford spans 250,000 years, it was the Romans who established the first permanent settlement alongside the River Darent at Dartford. Roman Dartford, probably no larger than a hamlet, lay on the main road connecting Londinium (London) with the channel ports. By 1086, when the Normans compiled Domesday Book, the Royal Manor of Tarentfort (Dartford - the crossing place over the River Darent) was a thriving agricultural community with a church (Holy Trinity), three chapels, a mill and a wharf on the River Darent. In Medieval times, Dartford grew into a recognisable market town with shops, inns, a priory and accommodation for the thousands of pilgrims who passed through Dartford on their way to Rochester and Canterbury. The reputation of the growing town was enhanced in the 1540s when Henry VIII commissioned the construction of a Royal Manor House – later the home of Anne of Cleves.

It was during Victorian times that Dartford became a town in the fullest sense of the word. The population increased almost ten-fold between 1800 and 1900. Dartford experienced its own mini industrial revolution due mainly to the arrival of the railway in 1849. Thousands of workers were needed in local industries and new companies were established or re-located to Dartford. Consequently, there was a boom in house building in Dartford between 1860 and 1890. A planned suburb, known as "New Town" was built to the north of East Hill. Churches, schools, hospitals, pubs, shops and leisure facilities were built to meet the needs of the fast-expanding population. The town still retained its links with local agriculture. There were a number of working farms close to the town; locally-grown hops were used in the town's two breweries and Dartford had busy cattle, corn and general markets.

The photographs in this book constitute an ephemeral record of a town and a way of life which is hardly recognisable today. The pace of change and development in twentieth-century Dartford has been rapid and far-reaching. Many of the town's old buildings have been replaced by more utilitarian structures; some main thoroughfares have been pedestrianised; some specialist small shops have disappeared and the layout of the late twentieth-century Dartford has been influenced by the needs of traffic management. One gets the impression that there was a great sense of community at the turn of the century, even though some of the residents lived in cramped conditions. Successive generations had lived, worked and shopped in the town and people felt rooted in its traditions. There was a prevailing sense of loyalty and local pride. The town was almost self-sufficient with its wide range of shops, services and facilities.

Walking the streets of Dartford today, one can perceive echoes of the past. Quaint buildings, old pubs and spacious parks co-exist with the modern developments. There are pockets of Dartford, backwaters, which have a distinctive ambience. The legacy of Victorian and Edwardian Dartford is particularly visible in the New Town area. Dartford has also preserved its role as a market town, attracting visitors from near and far. Future exciting developments are planned in and around the town, opening a new chapter in the story of an ever-changing urban landscape, giving Dartford a unique identity in North Kent.

One

The Town Centre

Looking east along the High Street, c.1904. The King's Head Inn, on the right, existed in Dartford as early as 1690 when John Woody was the proprietor. In 1851, the pub also included the property on the corner of Lowfield Street and was known as the King's Head County Hotel. The pub closed in the 1960s. Boots Cash Chemist is shown on the right.

The High Street, looking east, in 1909. Manning's fish shop, formerly the House of Correction, is on the right. Holy Trinity church in the background is Dartford's oldest building. It was built around 1080 by Bishop Gundulf, architect of the Tower of London. The church was an important centre for pilgrims in Medieval times.

High Street, Dartford

Further down the High Street at the same time. While the different methods of postcard reproduction suggest a different period a comparison of the fashions, means of transport and shops in the pictures reveals the truth.

Rush hour in the High Street, c.1915. Note the decorative "oil jars" above Mence Smith's hardware shop. These jars were the symbol of the hardware trade.

A similar view of the High Street in the late 1920s. The Cafe Devonia, Dartford's "High Class" restaurant, was above Burton's shop on the North side of the street. The roof-top "boxing ring" above the cafe was used by the adjacent Blackboy Inn as a look-out post during the days when stagecoaches frequented the town.

The High Street in the 1930s. The Cafe has borrowed an advertising technique from its neighbour (see above). Note the policeman on traffic duty. The Home and Colonial Stores, on the left, was trading as early as 1897 and was one of the many branches throughout Britain, specialising in the sale of tea, which followed the successful opening of the first branch in London, in 1885.

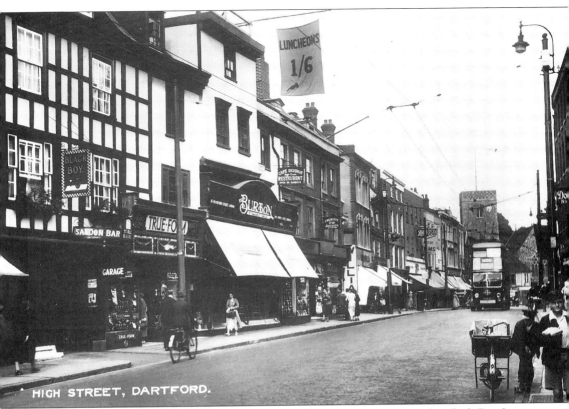

HIGH STREET, DARTFORD.

A 1950s view of the north side of the High Street. On the extreme left is the Black Boy Inn, formerly one of Dartford's premier coaching inns. The inn dates back to at least 1707 and was the meeting place of the Dartford Workhouse Trustees. In the nineteenth century, a scheduled coach service ran between the Black Boy and the Spur Inn at Borough, South London. The pub was demolished in 1966.

A view along the High Street in 1960. The Bull's Head, on the extreme left, was one of Dartford's oldest hostelries. It is listed in a document dated 1467. This old inn, which closed in

1972, was where Dartford's first branch of the Independent Order of Odd Fellows met.

Looking west along the High Street towards the junction of Spital Street and Hythe Street, c.1906. This view shows the Dartford branch of David Greig in the background.

Looking west along the High Street, c.1913. Snowden's stationers, printers and newsagents, on the right, traded in Dartford in the nineteenth century. The company was responsible for the publishing and printing of the West Kent Advertiser. Note the elaborate lamp-post. The lighting of street lamps in Dartford is first mentioned in 1771. The main thoroughfares were lit by gas as early as 1827. Dartford was amongst the pioneers of public gas supply in the United Kingdom.

Looking west towards Spital Street, c.1929. Note the policeman on point duty at "One Bell Corner". On the left is the One Bell Inn. The first pub on this site, known as "Le Bell" opened in 1508. An important hostelry in the eighteenth century, the pub survived as a local landmark at the junction of High Street and Lowfield Street until 1966. The name is commemorated in the modern-day " One Bell Corner", a spot where busy shoppers can relax and watch the world go by.

The High Street, looking west, c.1961. The Bull and George Hotel on the right has since been demolished to make way for a new Boots store. Jane Austen, the novelist, often stayed at this old coaching inn. On one occasion she nearly lost her precious writing box whilst staying at the inn. Left on a stagecoach bound for Gravesend, it was retrieved by a man on horseback, three miles down the road. The inn closed in 1972 and was demolished in 1981. Adjacent to the inn is "Teapot Penney's", one of Dartford's High Street landmarks.

The County Court and Wesleyan Methodist church buildings at the junction of Kent Road and Spital Street, c.1910. It is reputed that John Wesley, who often stayed at Bexley and Shoreham, preached in Dartford. Many of Dartford's leading eighteenth- and nineteenth-century industrialists were Methodists. The town still has two lively Methodist churches.

Spital Street, c.1926. On the right are the premises of R.H. Strickland, corn and seed merchants, which had its own wharf at Dartford Creek. The Coach and Horses pub in the background can be traced back to 1823, but may have existed as the Ship Inn as early as the 1740s.

Hythe Street, c.1913. On the right is F.C. Ward's barber's shop displaying the entrance. Note the ornate window sign advertising the fact that the shop undertook shaving.

The new post office in Hythe Street. One of Dartford's earliest post offices was situated in Lowfield Street. In 1926, a new post office opened in Hythe Street, this was rebuilt in 1972. The 1926 post office was equipped with offices, a staff dining room and kitchen, a telephone and telegraph room. Outbuildings were provided in the yard for motors, trucks and bicycles.

Terraced dwellings in Lowfield Street, c.1912. Dartford's hidden river, the Cran or Cranpit, flows parallel to Lowfield Street. Properties in this area were sometimes flooded when the water level was high. A thoroughfare known as "Lowfeld" existed in Medieval times - it led from Dartford to Wilmington.

Lowfield Street, c. 1913. "The Cinema", Dartford's first proper cinema (on the right) opened in 1913. It became known as the Rialto around 1926 and underwent another name change in the 1950's then it was known as the Century. The cinema finally closed in 1960.

Lowfield Street, looking towards One Bell Corner, c.1915. Martin's Bank on the right was flooded in the great flood of February 1900. Messrs Martin Ltd opened a branch in Lowfield Street on October 1, 1891, at the premises formerly occupied by a local carriage builder. The building is now occupied by Barclays Bank.

Lowfield Street (looking south), c.1919. On the left are Martin's Bank and the post office. Dartford's first post office was in the charge of a Mr John Hodges, who combined the duties of shoemaker with those of postmaster.

Dartford's memorial to those who died in the First World War. The ceremony of the unveiling and dedication of the memorial was conducted by Air Vice-Marshal Sir H. Geoffrey Salmond on 7 May 1922.

Two
Around Dartford

A view of Dartford from St Edmund's Burial Ground, c.1915. The upper burial ground was in use in the late eighteenth and nineteenth centuries. Some of the old gravestones have since been cleared to the periphery of the site, creating an attractive open space and leisure amenity. The site was formerly occupied by an ancient chantry or chapel dedicated to St Edmund. The nineteenth century Martyr's Memorial stands nearby.

Edwardian children enjoying the panoramic view across Dartford from St. Edmund's Burial Ground at the top of the "ninety-nine" (actually ninety-five) steps at East Hill.

The Martyr's Memorial, 1907, one of the most unusual memorials in Dartford. The first Martyr's Memorial was erected in the Upper Burial Ground in the 1850s. It commemorated Christopher Waid, a Protestant martyr, who was burned on Dartford Brent on July 17, 1555. Thousands of people flocked to Dartford from London and Kent to watch the burning. A new memorial was erected on the site in 1887 commemorating "Waid and two other Kent martyrs – Nicholas Hall and Margery Polley".

Shops on East Hill, 1908. Cycling was an enormously popular hobby around the turn of the century. Dartford had its own cycling club and a number of shops sold and repaired bicycles. E. Page's shop on East Hill advertised bicycles at £3-£13 each. W. E. Turner's shop sold groceries and sweets.

A traffic-free East Hill, c.1915. A number of small shops on East Hill served the needs of the local community.

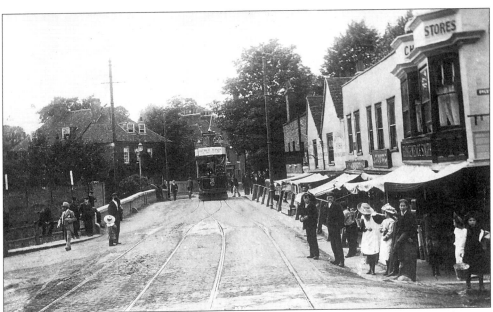

Tram No. 12 crossing the town bridge, watched by local children, c.1911. The row of quaint buildings on the right were known collectively as the "Chicken Run". On the right are the Bridge House premises of G. M. Smith's "Oil, Colour and Italian Stores". This well-known local shop sold tin and iron goods, woodware, mats, mops, brooms, brushes, leathers and sponges. Tin baths were often displayed on the outside of the shop.

The "Chicken Run", situated by the town bridge in Overy Liberty. The word "Overy" is an old abbreviated form of "over-the-river". In Medieval times, this part of Dartford was home to the town's leading merchants, and included property owned by the Guild of All Saints and Dartford Priory. A fulling mill (used for the cleaning and thickening of cloth) was sited in Overy Street amidst orchards and gardens. The "Chicken Run" was demolished in 1937.

Holy Trinity church from East Hill, c.1914. The Eleven Cricketers pub, on the right, reveals Dartford's close links with the game of cricket. The first recorded county match was played at Dartford in 1709. There was a pub on the site (known as the Queen's Head) as early as 1700 - it was renamed the Eleven Cricketers by 1778. The pub ceased trading in 1988.

East Hill, c.1940. Note the advert for Daren Bread baked from locally-milled flour. Dartford's trams had to negotiate the steep gradient of East Hill. Welsh non-slippery granite setts were used as a foundation for the tram tracks seen in the centre of this photograph.

Shops on the Brent, c.1914. The Brent was formerly an area of commonland used for the grazing of animals, and sport (including cricket) and public executions. The whole area was enclosed late in the nineteenth century and houses were built on the site. There was a great public outcry when the owner of the Dartford Gunpowder Mills requisitioned the traditional commonland and prevented public access, a right which had been enjoyed for centuries. Dartford Windmill stood in an elevated position on The Brent.

The Brent, c.1910. At this time trams and horse-drawn vehicles shared the same roads. Note the elaborate street lamp on the right.

St Alban's Road at the junction with Colney Road, c.1913. The functional "villas" lining this and similar roads in East Dartford were part of an 1870s development, known as "New Town", a purpose-built suburb of Dartford designed to house factory workers and the lower middle classes.

Watling Street, around 1915. Note the imposing ornamental iron street lamp in the middle of the road.

A view from Princes Road with Tree Estate in the background. This road, originally known as the Dartford Southern By-pass, was designed to provide employment for the large numbers of unemployed residents of Dartford and to ease the heavy congestion in central Dartford. The road was officially opened by H.R.H. The Prince of Wales on 19 November, 1924.

Charles Potter (the last Sexton of Dartford's cemeteries) and his family in the garden of the cemetery lodge at East Hill.

The No.8 tram making its way up West Hill, c.1907. On the left are the former Dartford Workhouse buildings which were taken over by the Dartford Board of Guardians in 1834 and later extended. The vagrant wards of the workhouse were considered to be some of the best in England. The buildings now occupy part of the West Hill Hospital site and have recently been restored.

Dartford Road at the junction with Lawrence Hill Road, c.1911. This view is taken looking west towards Crayford.

Highfield Road, c.1906. In 1889 this leafy residential area was described as "perhaps the most important residential locality". Earlier, in 1872, the unmade road surface was described as "a swamp".

Highfield Road, c.1906, shows a total lack of traffic. Local children were able to play games in the street with little fear of being run over. The occasional horse and cart made deliveries to local houses. Horse manure made roads slippery and rather smelly in summer.

Houses in Summerhill Road, c.1915. Some of the earliest properties in this road date from the 1860s.

Miskin Road, c.1907. These large town "villas" housed some of Dartford's more affluent residents. Note the neat trellis-style fencing. In 1891, the Dartford Local Board awarded a contract for the renovation of Miskin Road which had fallen into bad repair. The Miskin family played a prominent part in the life of the town. William Miskin, a respected local businessman and philanthropist was a member of the Local Board of Health.

Shepherds Lane, c.1920. The original Shepherds Lane was wide, rough track which led to Dartford Heath. Some of the properties in Shepherds Lane were built in the 1880s.

Tower Road, c.1904. Portland Cottages, the first buildings in Tower Road were constructed around 1860. Note the railings fronting the houses and the solitary gas lamp.

Heathside, Dartford Heath, c.1905.

MAYPOLE HOUSE DARTFORD HEATH.   F.K. 243

Maypole House, Dartford Heath, c.1910.

Wilmington Grange, Dartford Heath, c.1913.

Oakfield Lane, c.1915. This shady, tranquil lane led to Madame Osterberg's College of Physical Education which moved to Dartford from Hampstead in 1895.

A pair of "villas" for sale at King Edward Avenue, c.1908.

Artistic semi-detached houses at Priory Park, available for sale in 1908. These houses are typical of the Edwardian era, well-built and appealing to the middle classes. The Priory Park Estate (King Edward Avenue) was built between 1906 and 1908.

Three

Education, Religion and Healthcare

Dartford Grammar School for Girls (formerly known as the County School for Girls) was built to accommodate 425 girls. The school was originally based at the Technical Institute in Essex Road. The school buildings were formally opened in October 1912.

County School for Girls, Dartford. The Art Room.

The Art Room at the County School for Girls.

The Botany Laboratory at the County School for Girls.

The library at the County School for Girls.

Dartford Boy's Grammar School, c.1906. The Grammar School was founded in 1576 and was originally based in a schoolroom over the Market House in the High Street. The present building, designed by the architect Sir Arthur Blomfield, was erected in 1866. Famous old boys include Sir Erasmus Wilson, Sir Henry Havelock and Mick Jagger. Note the horse trough in the road outside the school.

Playing fields at Dartford Boy's Grammar School, c.1908. In 1905 new science, art and form rooms were constructed in the east side of the school at a cost of £5,000. The buildings, part-funded by voluntary subscriptions, were opened by Colonel Kidd on 22 June 1905.

Pupils in Standard I at Westgate Road School. Note the old wooden desks, school slate and pottery ink-wells.

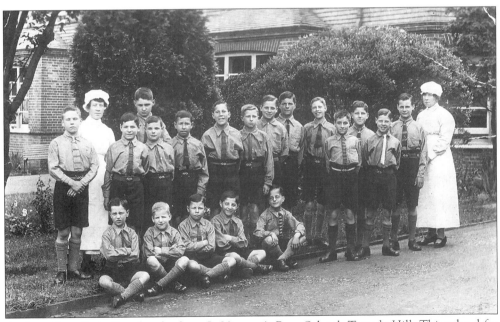

A class of pupils, believed to be from St Vincent's Boys School, Temple Hill. This school for Roman Catholic boys, was originally established at Tanner's Hill, Deptford in 1872 and moved to Dartford in 1875. The school was under the superintendence of the Presentation Brothers, a self-denying religious community. Attached to the school was a farm and garden where the boys received instruction in both farming and gardening.

Students playing lacrosse at Madame Osterberg's Physical Training College, which moved from London to Oakfield Lane in 1895. Madame Osterberg pioneered the teaching of physical training to young women and her college was the first of its kind in Britain. The game of netball was invented at the college as was the gymslip, worn by generations of schoolgirls.

Madame Osterberg's Physical Training College at Dartford, c.1910. College students were encouraged to undertake all kinds of sport and physical exercise. The college had its own cycle track and outdoor gymnasium. Famous old girls include Ann Packer (gold medallist in the Tokyo Olympics), Rachael Heyhoe Flint, former Captain of the England women's cricket team and Jean Harris, tennis coach and writer. The site is now occupied by the University of Greenwich.

The Technical Institute, Essex Road, c.1913. This building, which housed Dartford's first public museum, opened in 1902, due mainly to the efforts of the Dartford Free Lecture Society. A wide range of day and evening courses was available at the Technical Institute. The building (now Enterprise House) is still standing.

The Dartford Board School, West Hill, c.1905. This school opened in January 1891. It was attended by 233 boys and 382 girls and infants. The school buildings look very much the same today.

St Ursula's High School for Young Ladies stood at the top of West Hill and later became Our Lady's High School (until 1963). This photograph dates from around 1912. All of the old buildings have been demolished but Our Lady's Junior School stands close to the site of the old school.

Dartford National School, West Hill, c.1910. The National School opened in 1826 and was described by John Dunkin, local antiquarian, as a "somewhat tasty structure". The school accommodated 200 boys and 140 girls in the nineteenth century. The schoolmaster lived on the premises. The school (now Holy Trinity) relocated to a new site in West Dartford. At present, the school buildings are derelict and the site is due for redevelopment.

Darenth Asylum Schools, c.1908. An industrial training colony was established at the hospital to provide training in "useful work" for inmates with learning difficulties. The hospital at Darenth earned an international reputation as a centre of excellence undertaking pioneering work with patients.

Highfield Road Baptist chapel, c.1913. Dartford's first recorded Baptist church was situated in the High Street. The Highfield Road chapel, which accommodated a congregation of 450, was built by local builder James Sharp in 1868. The Revd Alfred Sturge was the first pastor.

The Wesleyan (Methodist) church, Spital Street. The church opened on 27 May 1845 and was extended in 1869 and 1910. Methodists were active in Dartford as early as 1758. John Hall, who established the Dartford ironworks in 1785, was the principal founder of the first Wesleyan church in Dartford. He converted two cottages in Waterside into a church which opened on New Year's Day, 1794.

Congregational Church, Dartford

The Congregational church (now United Reformed) in West Hill. Dartford's Congregationalists first met in an iron church erected on a site in Dartford Road in 1870. This church building dates from 1882.

Members of the Dartford Salvation Army Band in 1907, outside the old fire station which has since been demolished. The Salvation Army arrived in Dartford in October 1886, with a

barracks in Overy Street. The Hythe Street Citadel was opened in 1912.

The exterior of St Anselm's Catholic church, Spital Street, demolished to make way for the construction of the Arndale (Priory) shopping centre. A Catholic centre or "Mission" was opened here in 1866 by the Capuchin Fathers of Greenhithe. The church, which opened in December 1900, was the gift of E.J. Fooks of Chislehurst, whose father's house used to stand on the same site.

The interior of St Anselm's Catholic church, c.1947. The church was built in the plain Early English style from the plans of F.A. Walters.

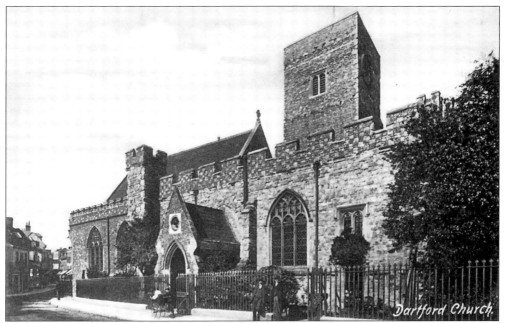

Holy Trinity church, c.1905. Set beside the River Darent and with an imposing Norman tower, Holy Trinity is Dartford's best known landmark and oldest building. In 1415 Henry V stopped at Dartford for a thanksgiving service in this church when travelling to London after his triumph at Agincourt. After his death in France, Henry's body lay overnight at Holy Trinity for a requiem mass before continuing on its way to Westminster Abbey.

The interior of Holy Trinity church, c.1920. A superb fifteenth-century painting of St George slaying the dragon occupies one of the walls. Memorials in the church commemorate Sir John Spielman who founded England's first commercially viable paper mill in Dartford; Richard Trevithick, inventor of the steam locomotive, who died at the Bull Inn, Dartford in 1833; and William D'eath, one of the founders of Dartford Grammar School.

The Vicarage, sited next to the River Darent, was damaged when the river flooded parts of the town in 1866. Ralph de Wingeham was the first recorded Vicar of Dartford (around 1174).

A local church choir in the late 1920s.

Members of the local branch of the Church Army, photographed outside St Mary's church, Stone, in 1910.

The Martyr's Memorial Hall, West Hill, was the meeting place of the Dartford Young Men's Bible Class (founded in 1883). In 1928, the building became the headquarters of the Y.M.C.A. Later, on 3 December 1930, H.R.H. Princess Helena Victoria opened the new extension to the building. The Y.M.C.A. is still thriving in Dartford at its modern centre on West Hill.

Once part of the Dartford workhouse, the King Edward Hospital (now West Hill) became an important hospital in north west Kent. Vickers & Co. took over the hospital during the First World War and extended the facilities to include a massage and electrical clinic. The hospital was badly bombed during the Second World War, one of the worst incidents occurring in September 1940, when a high explosive bomb demolished two women's wards, killing a nurse and twenty-four patients.

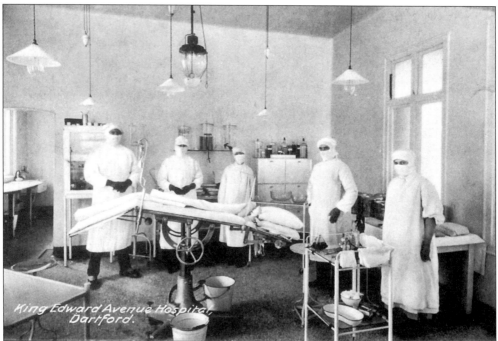

The operating theatre and sterilising room at King Edward Avenue Hospital, c.1919. The Workhouse Board of Guardians assumed control of the hospital in 1919 but handed it over to the Public Assistance Committee in 1929.

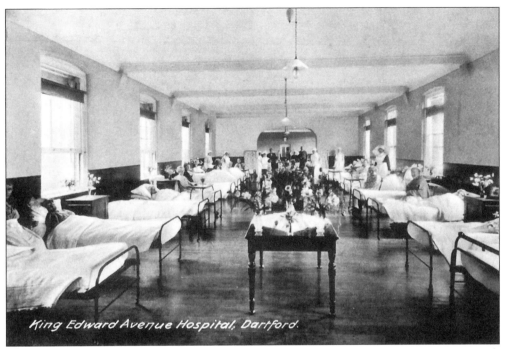

The newly refurbished women's ward at the King Edward Avenue Hospital, c.1919. The wards were clean, neat and simply furnished.

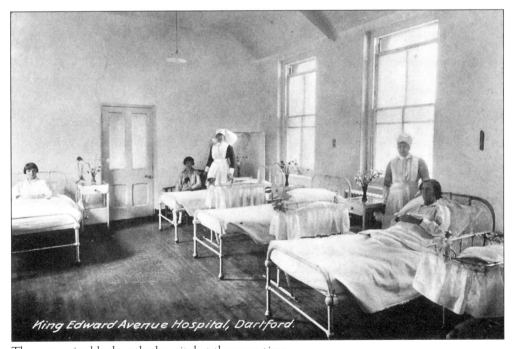

The maternity block at the hospital at the same time.

Joyce Green Hospital was opened in December 1902 to provide appropriate emergency accommodation for smallpox and fever victims. In 1901-2 two temporary hospitals, the Long Reach and the Orchard were erected adjacent to the Joyce Green Hospital, to deal with the smallpox epidemic of that time.

The entrance to the Third Australian Auxiliary Hospital (Orchard Hospital) at Long Reach on the Dartford marshes, c.1915.

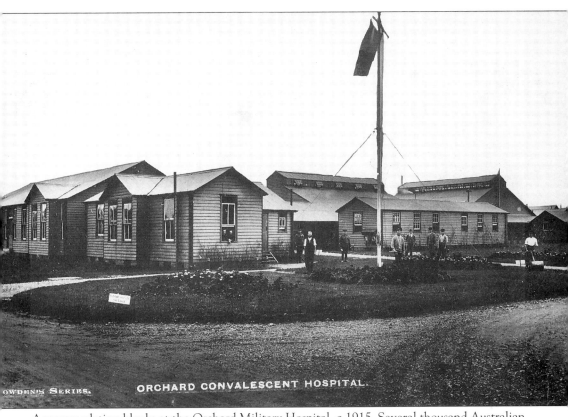

OWDEN'S SERIES. ORCHARD CONVALESCENT HOSPITAL.

Accommodation blocks at the Orchard Military Hospital, c.1915. Several thousand Australian troops were treated at this hospital between 1915 and 1919. Dartford residents welcomed the Australians into their homes and organised entertainments for them. Some of the Australians married Dartford girls.

Some of the patients and soldiers at the hospital, with the accommodation blocks in the background.

ital.

Snowden's Series.

The Metropolitan Asylum at Darenth, later known as Darenth Park Hospital. The hospital's two water towers, each around 100 feet high, were once a conspicuous local landmark. The hospital buildings are currently in the course of demolition.

Livingstone Cottage Hospital, East Hill, c.1907. The memorial stone was laid on 21 April 1894 by H. M. Stanley, the African explorer. Mr Stanley's speech lasted over an hour. The hospital was paid for by public subscription. Mr Silas M. Burroughs started the subscription list with a donation of £1,000. The first patient was admitted in December 1894 and electric lighting was installed in 1901. The Livingstone Hospital is still open, continuing to make a valuable contribution to community health care.

Lowfield Street, c.1906. On the left of the photograph are the Lowfield Street Almshouses. These were rebuilt in 1889, replacing Elizabethan Almshouses.

Long Reach Isolation Hospital. The earliest patients were treated aboard hulks moored in the River Thames. The hulks were replaced by the land-based hospital which was eventually demolished in 1975.

Staff and soldiers employed in the Steward's Stores at the War Hospital in 1918. Note the meat hanging on the doors. The sign at the rear of the food and drinks display reads "Work like Hell and Be Merry".

Royal Army Medical Corps soldiers based at the Dartford War Hospital during the First World War.

Four

At Work

Burroughs, Wellcome & Co.'s pharmaceutical works at Dartford, c.1905. The internationally-famous business moved to Dartford from Wandsworth in 1889. The Dartford works were originally known as the Phoenix Mills. For over a century, the company has manufactured a wide range of products for the diagnosis, prevention and treatment of disease.

Burroughs, Wellcome & Co.'s factory site at Dartford, c.1905. Note the impressive size of Dartford's former Mill Pond. The Wellcome Foundation, recently taken over by Glaxo, is the town's largest single employer. The importance of management-staff relations was recognised from the start and an eight-hour day was adopted in the opening of the Dartford works. Catering for the staff commenced in 1905. The Wellcome Club and Institute at Acacia Hall, one of the first staff clubs in the country, was opened in 1899.

Keyes' or Hard's Mill on the River Darent. The river which flows through Dartford had been used to drive mill wheels since Saxon times. Dartford's first known mill is recorded in Domesday Book (1086). The upper storeys were demolished in the 1930s but the ground floor still exists and is now used by the Royal Air Force Association.

View in Powder Mill Grounds, Dartford.

A view into the grounds of the Powder Mill on the River Darent, c.1907. The production of gunpowder commenced on the Bignores site in 1732 and continued until 1907. By the nineteenth century, Dartford had become one of the three largest producers of gunpowder in this country. The government would have been hard pushed for ammunition during the Crimean War had it not been for these mills. The site of the mills has been excavated and their remains can be seen at Powder Mill Lane.

David Greig, provision merchant, at the junction of Hythe Street and Spital Street, c.1910. Note the delivery bicycle parked outside the shop. David Greig, part of a national chain of shops, later had premises in Lowfield Street.

Daren Mill, Hythe Street, c.1920. The business was first established by Leonard Keyes in 1875, at the Brent windmill, moving to the Daren Mills on Dartford Creek in 1891. The firm, which had an impressive fleet of delivery vehicles, specialised in the manufacture of white flour, Daren biscuits and self-raising flour, the latter being produced by Seraflo Ltd, a subsidiary company.

Inspecting printed fabric for flaws at Warner and Sons Ltd Printing Works, Home Gardens, in the 1930s. The print works were demolished in the 1980s. Hand-block printing of textiles commenced at the print works on the River Darent in 1865.

71

A trade display mounted by J. Salway and Sons Ltd, Lowfield Street, c.1945. This well known local company manufactured the ornamental iron gates at the entrance to Hesketh Park and

the ornamental balustrading in the Co-op building which opened at Spital Street in July 1935.

Lunchtime at J. & E. Hall's foundry. After 1907, many of the workers were able to travel home to lunch, thanks to the installation of Dartford's tramway system.

The North Pole, c.1907. This splendid building and local landmark (recently demolished) was the brainchild of Everard Hesketh, Managing Director of J. & E. Hall Ltd. It opened in 1902 as a temperance restaurant, providing cheap meals for the company's workforce. After 1907, the building was used as offices. J. & E. Hall specialised in the manufacture of refrigeration equipment, hence the name of the building. The Polar Bear weather vane, which surmounted the building and provided a target for local youths with air rifles, was rescued when the building was demolished and is now on permanent display at Dartford Museum.

One of the workshops at J. & E. Halls. The company, which had a humble beginning in 1784, diversified into all sorts of areas, including the manufacture of gunpowder milling machinery, steam engines, refrigeration units for ships, lifts and chassis for heavy motor vehicles. The company is still based in Dartford as part of the APV group of companies.

J. & E. Hall's trade stand at the Royal Lancashire Show in the mid-1950s. The glamorous ladies were known as the "Television Toppers".

" The Canal" at Dartford, c.1960. The River Darent was navigable from Dartford Creek to its confluence with the River Thames. Barges were employed to transport materials to and from the riverside factories, mills and warehouses, Dartford Creek was straightened in 1840. The creek was a favourite place for swimming and fishing.

Barges on Dartford Creek, c.1910. In 1835 a group of local entrepreneurs pressed for the canalisation of Dartford Creek. A Bill for the "Making of a Ship Canal from Dartford to the River Thames" was rejected by Parliament. However the Navigation Commissioners were empowered to shorten the creek by around three quarters of a mile to allow barges of over 200 tons to navigate the extreme head of the creek.

The Daily Telegraph paper mills. This mill was built in 1862-3 under the trading name of the Ettrick Forest Mill. It closed in 1866, but re-opened as the Daily Telegraph mills in 1867. Over 130 houses were built in Dartford to provide accommodation for the workforce.

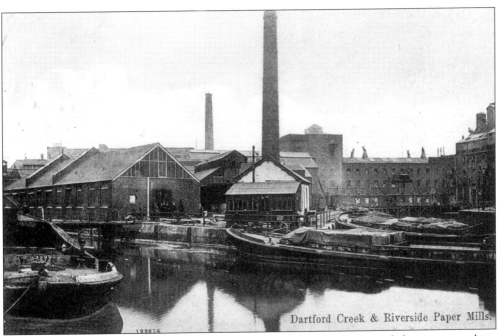

Dartford Creek and Riverside paper mills, c.1911. These mills housed five paper-making machines with a production of around 250 tons per week. In 1909, the mills, which employed 500 people were taken over by Messrs Albert E. Reed & Co. Ltd.

Workmen laying tramlines in Hythe Street close to the railway arch, c.1905. The idea of establishing tramways in Dartford was first proposed in 1900. Construction work began in 1905 and the official opening took place on 14 February 1906. Twelve double-decker tramcars carried over two million passengers during the first year of operation.

Dartford tramcars decorated for the official opening of the Dartford Light Railways, 14 February 1906. In the early hours of Tuesday 8 August 1917, the tram depot in Burnham Road was destroyed by fire. Thirteen tramcars were destroyed before the fire could be extinguished.

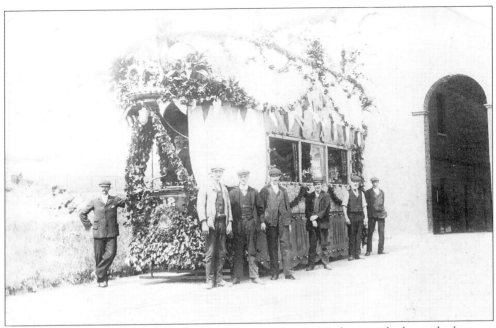

A Dartford tramcar decorated for the Coronation of George V, photographed outside the tram depot in Burnham Road.

HIGH ST. TRAM CENTRE, DARTFORD.

The "Tram Centre", outside the Bull Hotel, c.1920. This view is towards Spital Street. The tram tracks passed through the centre of Dartford, connecting with the tram system operated by Bexley and Erith. The tracks also served the parishes of Crayford, Wilmington and Stone. After the tramcar depot was destroyed by fire in 1917, Bexley Council agreed to run their trams over the Dartford track and the service was maintained.

Mr W. Underhill of Underhill and Sons Fruiterers of Dartford, close to the Victoria mill, East Hill. Flour from this mill was delivered once a week to Windsor Castle for use in the Royal kitchens and bakery. Queen Victoria issued her personal warrant to the mill which held the Royal appointment for the supply of flour.

A horse-drawn delivery cart used by A. Canty, tobacco and cigar merchants of Spital Street.

A horse-drawn delivery waggon belonging to Penney, Son and Parker, local grocers. The waggon was presumably decorated for entry in a carnival procession. The horse and dog are wearing unusual headgear!

Delivering beer to the Welcome All pub at Horns Cross near Dartford. The lorry, owned by Kidd's brewery was a Hallford, manufactured by J. & E. Hall, c.1916.

An early view of Dartford station. The railway came to Dartford on 30 July 1849 with the construction of a line from London to Rochester via Woolwich, Dartford and Gravesend. The railway through Eltham, Sidcup and Bexley, which had always been known as the Loop Line, was opened on 1 September 1866 and the line to Dartford through Bexleyheath on 1 May 1895.

The railway sidings, c.1910. This nostalgic view of the sidings is a reminder that Dartford was once part of the "Age of Steam". Richard Trevithick, inventor of the steam locomotive lived, died and is buried in Dartford. The first electrically driven trains between Charing Cross and Dartford began running in June 1926.

W.H. Smith's newsagents at the station in 1913. It was important that commuters should have plenty to read as the journey from Dartford to Charing Cross via Blackheath took one hour and eleven minutes!

Dartford Junction station complete with ornate gas lamps. By the 1930s, nearly 400 trains stopped here daily.

The Dartford Volunteer Fire Brigade in Kent Road in 1896. The County Court and the Armoury are visible in the background. Dartford had a manual fire engine as early as 1740. A charge of six shillings (30p) was made each time the engine was called out. In 1827 an engine house was constructed adjoining the parish church. It was not until 1902 that a full fire station was built in Overy Street (now demolished). The new steam fire engine cost £400.

Dartford police, Highfield Road, c.1920-1. Prior to the 1850s, Dartford was patrolled by part-time constables employed by the parish. The remains of the old town "lock-up" can still be seen close to the entrance to West Hill Hospital. A proper police station was erected in 1866, under the auspices of the Kent County Constabulary. By 1903, Dartford was served by four officers and ten constables.

Five

Leisure

Members of Dartford Football Club for the 1904-5 season.

During the First World War, Dartford Amateur Football Club took the opportunity to play against members of one of the town's anti-aircraft gun crews. Anti-aircraft guns were sited on the Brent, the Heath and the Marshes.

Members of the Dartford Harriers in the 1920s. The Harriers are still very active in the town, making use of the running track in Central Park.

Members of the J. & E. Hall men's hockey team for the 1927-8 season. A number of local companies actively encouraged their staff to participate in sports activities.

Above and below: Westgate House, the former home of the Hall family, c.1909. This imposing building later housed the Dartford Working Men's Club and Institute. One famous visitor was the Prince of Wales who attended a dance in 1928. Facilities included a library, billiards room and hot and cold baths.

Members of J. & E. Hall's boxing section 1934-5. Dartford Marshes were the scene of bare-fisted prize fights in the nineteenth century. Train-loads of spectators travelled from London to Dartford to watch the illegal fights which were rarely halted by the local constabulary. A fatality occurred at a fight at Long Reach in 1872.

Dartford's roller skating rink in Spital Street (now part of the site occupied by Beadle's Garage), c.1910. The young Winston Churchill and A.J. Balfour both addressed huge crowds here in here

Members of the Dartford Alpine Glee Party in 1905.

Members of the Wellcome Club and Institute at their fancy dress dance, 7 February 1908. The club was opened at Acacia Hall in 1899 by Sir Henry Wellcome for the use of the company's employees as recreation rooms and pleasure grounds. The Wellcome Foundation's annual garden party has been one of the social highlights of the summer for many years.

The St Vincent's Boys' School Military Band, 1912. The school, for poor Catholic boys moved to Temple Hill from Deptford in 1875.

Francis Howard and his Accordion Dance Band, presumed to be one of many groups of entertainers who gave concerts in the Dartford area earlier this century. The picture was taken by Pyefinch and Swaine, Dartford-based photographers.

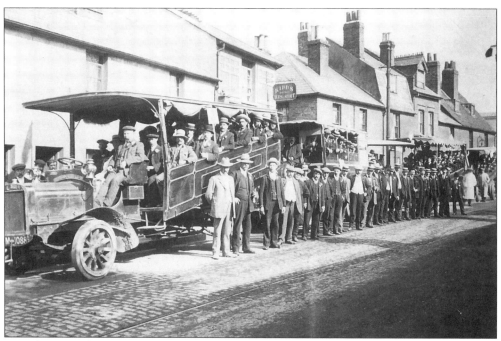

A works outing for J. & E. Hall employees, c.1910. The sign in the background advertises Kidd's bottled ales and stout. Kidd's brewery stood on the site now occupied by the Dartford Co-op store.

A children's outing outside the Fulwich Hall, St Vincent's Road, c.1920.

A pub outing outside the Ivy Leaf pub, Darenth Road, c.1927. The old Ivy Leaf, shown in this photograph was rebuilt in 1929 in mock-Tudor style.

A works outing for the staff of Warner and Sons Ltd, fabric printers of Home Gardens, June 1930.

The Bull Hotel, High Street, c.1910. This is Dartford's oldest inn, possibly dating back to the fourteenth century, when it was known as the "Hole Bull" (the Holy Seal) and owned by the nuns of Dartford Priory. Queen Victoria is reputed to have stayed at the inn in 1838.

The Crown and Anchor Inn (now the Wat Tyler) at the junction of High Street and Bullace Lane. The timber-framed building is Medieval c.1416 and formed part of a much larger house which was partially demolished in 1955. There is no real evidence to prove that this was once the home of Wat Tyler, who led the Peasant's Revolt in 1381.

The Orange Tree Inn, Hawley Road, c.1915. This building dates from the seventeenth century, when it was known as Orange Tree Farm. It was an inn by 1832 and in 1904 was sold to the Dartford Brewery Company, based in Lowfield Street.

The Horse and Groom pub, Leyton Cross Road, c.1930. The building is Georgian but the history of the pub can only be traced back as far as 1879. The pub is a favourite stopping-off place for visitors to Dartford Heath.

The Bandstand, Central Park, c.1905. The park, known as the "Dartford Central Recreation Ground", was opened to the public in June 1905, by the donor Lt.-Col. C.N. Kidd. More land was added to the park at a later date.

The bowling green, Central Park, c.1905. On the left are the buildings of the Dartford Brewery Company.

The croquet lawn, Central Park, c.1905. Note the ornamental water-course in the foreground. Today the park houses such curiosities as some Roman paving cobbles from Watling Street, part of a Roman wall from Farningham and one of the arches of the original thirteenth century footbridge over the River Darent which was removed when the Town Bridge was widened in 1921. It has been re-erected with the addition of "modern" parapets.

Central Park, showing the ornamental pond and tennis courts on the right. The park still attracts a wide variety of wildlife, including foxes, grass snakes and kingfishers.

The "lake" and grounds of Hesketh Park, the gift of Mr Everard Hesketh who purchased part of the Brent to be laid out as a pleasure garden and cricket ground.

The bandstand, Hesketh Park, c.1910.

The children's corner at Hesketh Park, c.1906. The park still has a children's playground which is a popular meeting place for local youngsters.

A cricket match in progress at Hesketh Park in the 1960s. County cricket matches were played at Hesketh Park until the early 1980s.

A view of the River Darent from the Town Bridge, c.1905. A special riverside path has now been created which enables ramblers to walk along the Darent Valley from Dartford to Sevenoaks.

The River Darent, seen flowing through Central Park, has always been an important wildlife habitat. The channel and banks of the river have been altered to reduce the likelihood of flooding.

The old Mill Stream at Dartford, c.1955. This was a favourite spot for local fishermen.

The Avenue, Brooklands, c.1909.

Brooklands on the River Darent, c.1905.

Brooklands Bridge, c.1936. A picturesque spot on the River Darent.

Brooklands Lake. This old flooded gravel pit offers an attractive recreational amenity close to the centre of the town. The lake is another popular haunt with anglers.

THE DONKEYS, DARTFORD HEATH.

Dartford Heath has long offered facilities for recreation and leisure. Once the home of the Dartford Warbler, parts of the heath were still used for the grazing of animals at the beginning of the twentieth century. These donkeys were "put out to grass" on the heath.

Six

Events

The Great Flood of Dartford, February 1900. Dartford's history had been punctuated by bad floods, the last of which happened in 1968, when much of the town centre was submerged under flood water. In 1968, boats were rowed up Dartford High Street! Measures have since been taken to eliminate the threat.

High Street flooded in 1900. Many of the town's shops and public buildings were badly damaged by the flood water. The local council chartered a number of carts and vehicles to convey residents from one side of the town to the other. It was reported that Dartford resembled "a modern Venice"!

Dartford Fire Brigade pumping out the flooded cellars of the Bull Hotel during the flood of 1900. The pub had recently had new cellars built, these were badly damaged, along with a lot of valuable stock.

Looking east along the High Street from "Pump Corner" where the town's water pump stood. The streets were decorated to celebrate the Coronation of King Edward VII in June 1902.

The premises of James Sharp and Sons, Hythe Street, Dartford, decorated for the 1902 Coronation. This was one of the oldest established businesses in Dartford and was originally founded by James Sharp Snr. in 1800 as a builder and timber merchant. The Baltic Saw Mills were later added to the business.

Looking west along the Coronation-decorated High Street.

Boy scouts and bandsmen parading through Dartford, possibly to celebrate the Coronation of George V in 1911.

Dartford High Street, looking east, decorated for George V's coronation on June 22 1911. The large chimney to the right displays the words "Bull Inn" in the decorative brickwork. Note the advert for Daren Bread made from flour milled in Dartford.

J. & E. Hall's Hythe Street buildings decorated for the Coronation of George V.

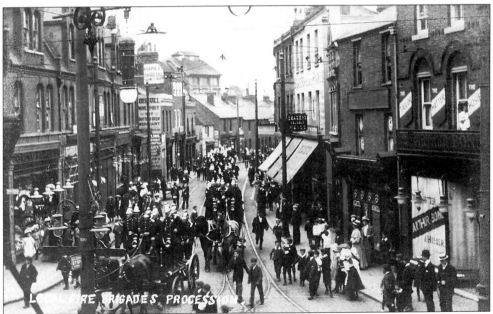

A spectacular parade of horse-drawn fire engines passing through Dartford – possibly to celebrate the Coronation of George V. Dartford acquired its first motor (Merryweather) fire engine in 1912.

A group of locals "Beating the Bounds" near the boundary marker in Maiden Lane, May 1913.

"Beating the Bounds" near the Gunpowder Mills.

"Beating the Bounds" outside the Long Reach Tavern. This isolated Thames-side pub was another ideal venue for bare-fist fighting. The pub existed as early as 1801 and closed in the 1960s. It was busy during the heyday of Joyce Green Aerodrome, used for training by the Royal Flying Corps up to and during the First World War.

Members of Dartford Grammar School's Officer Training Corps at camp in 1911.

Members of the First Woolwich Cadet Corps camping at Dartford, c.1905. Note the large bell-tents.

Church parade for members of the Fifth London Brigade on or near Dartford Heath in 1908.

A contingent of soldiers marching through Dartford, possibly after a church parade on the Heath.

Madam Butterfly and her attendants. Part of the Peace Celebrations held at the Dartford War Hospital at the end of the First World War.

More peace celebrations at the hospital.

The thirty-fourth company of the Royal Army Medical Corps Band, based at the hospital in 1918.

The First World War Roll of Honour for Great Queen Street, Little Queen Street and Gladstone Road.

Central Park flooded when the River Darent burst its banks, 4 January 1925. Almost the whole area from the War Memorial to the grounds of the Glentworth Club was submerged, in some places to a depth of two-and-a-half feet. Cellars in Lowfield Street and the High Street had to be pumped out.

On 13 September 1933, Dartford received its Charter of Incorporation. The Lord Mayor of London delivered the Charter document to Dartford amidst great celebrations in the town. The Lord Mayor's coach arrived at the boundary of Dartford to be greeted by the High Sheriff of Kent and the Charter Mayor and Mayoress of Dartford.

Part of the procession of carriages at Dartford's Charter Day celebrations in Market Street. Thousands watched the procession and the evening pageant, entitled "Dartford in the Making".

Looking west along a High Street decorated for the coronation of George VI, 12 May 1937. The Crown and Anchor Inn (now the Wat Tyler) is on the right, adjacent to A. Phillips and Co.'s bicycle shop.

The band of the eighteenth Battalion Home Guard outside the Drill Hall adjoining Central Park, 1943. Some of the band members were as young as fourteen. In 1943 the average age of

Home Guard members was only 29, as many teenagers had joined. All the instruments used by the bandsmen were paid for by local companies.

Employees of John C. Beadle, Spital Street, who were also serving members of Dartford's Home Guard during the Second World War. Of the Dartford Battalion, Colonel A.A.E. Chitty said "I haven't seen a smarter Home Guard parade in all of Kent, they are smarter than many regular units' parades".

A Victory Party at Home Gardens in 1945. VE Day was a great occasion of joy for adults and children alike. Street parties were organised throughout Dartford – rationing points were pooled and stores raided. In the evening bonfires were lit in the middle of local roads. These bonfires left large round burnt patches in the road surfaces and were a visible sign of the celebrations for many years.

A Victory Party in Lawford Gardens, 1945. These children were treated to fruit jelly and ice cream.

A fancy dress competition organised as part of the Victory Party held at Colney Road in 1945. Note the wounded soldier in the front row!

To finish, there follows a selection of comic postcards overprinted with the name "Dartford", dating from 1907. Cards of this type were available in many towns throughout Britain, printed and distributed by the Cynicus Publishing Company of Tayport, Fife, Scotland.

The Lovers' Walk
The Dell, Dartford Heath

Stock List

(Titles are listed according to the pre-1974 county boundaries)

BERKSHIRE

Wantage
Irene Hancock
ISBN 0-7524-0146 7

CARDIGANSHIRE

Aberaeron and Mid Ceredigion
William Howells
ISBN 0-7524-0106-8

CHESHIRE

Ashton-under-Lyne and Mossley
Alice Lock
ISBN 0-7524-0164-5

Around Bebington
Pat O'Brien
ISBN 0-7524-0121-1

Crewe
Brian Edge
ISBN 0-7524-0052-5

Frodsham and Helsby
Frodsham and District Local History Group
ISBN 0-7524-0161-0

Macclesfield Silk
Moira Stevenson and Louanne Collins
ISBN 0-7524-0315 X

Marple
Steve Cliffe
ISBN 0-7524-0316-8

Runcorn
Bert Starkey
ISBN 0-7524-0025-8

Warrington
Janice Hayes
ISBN 0-7524-0040-1

West Kirby to Hoylake
Jim O'Neil
ISBN 0-7524-0024-X

Widnes
Anne Hall and the Widnes Historical Society
ISBN 0-7524-0117-3

CORNWALL

Padstow
Malcolm McCarthy
ISBN 0-7524-0033-9

St Ives Bay
Jonathan Holmes
ISBN 0-7524-0186-6

COUNTY DURHAM

Bishop Auckland
John Land
ISBN 0-7524-0312-5

Around Shildon
Vera Chapman
ISBN 0-7524-0115-7

CUMBERLAND

Carlisle
Dennis Perriam
ISBN 0-7524-0166-1

DERBYSHIRE

Around Alfreton
Alfreton and District Heritage Trust
ISBN 0-7524-0041-X

Barlborough, Clowne, Creswell and Whitwell
Les Yaw
ISBN 0-7524-0031-2

Around Bolsover
Bernard Haigh
ISBN 0-7524-0021-5

Around Derby
Alan Champion and Mark Edworthy
ISBN 0-7524-0020-7

Long Eaton
John Barker
ISBN 0-7524-0110-6

Ripley and Codnor
David Buxton
ISBN 0-7524-0042-8

Shirebrook
Geoff Sadler
ISBN 0-7524-0028-2

Shirebrook: A Second Selection
Geoff Sadler
ISBN 0-7524-0317-6

DEVON

Brixham
Ted Gosling and Lyn Marshall
ISBN 0-7524-0037-1

Around Honiton
Les Berry and Gerald Gosling
ISBN 0-7524-0175-0

Around Newton Abbot
Les Berry and Gerald Gosling
ISBN 0-7524-0027-4

Around Ottery St Mary
Gerald Gosling and Peter Harris
ISBN 0-7524-0030-4

Around Sidmouth
Les Berry and Gerald Gosling
ISBN 0-7524-0137-8

DORSET

Around Uplyme and Lyme Regis
Les Berry and Gerald Gosling
ISBN 0-7524-0044-4

ESSEX

Braintree and Bocking
John and Sandra Adlam and Mark Charlton
ISBN 0-7524-0129-7

Ilford
Ian Dowling and Nick Harris
ISBN 0-7524-0050-9

Ilford: A Second Selection
Ian Dowling and Nick Harris
ISBN 0-7524-0320-6

Saffron Walden
Jean Gumbrell
ISBN 0-7524-0176-9

GLAMORGAN

Around Bridgend
Simon Eckley
ISBN 0-7524-0189-0

Caerphilly
Simon Eckley
ISBN 0-7524-0194-7

Around Kenfig Hill and Pyle
Keith Morgan
ISBN 0-7524-0314-1

The County Borough of Merthyr Tydfil
Carolyn Jacob, Stephen Done and Simon Eckley
ISBN 0-7524-0012-6

Mountain Ash, Penrhiwceiber and Abercynon
Bernard Baldwin and Harry Rogers
ISBN 0-7524-0114-9

Pontypridd
Simon Eckley
ISBN 0-7524-0017-7

Rhondda
Simon Eckley and Emrys Jenkins
ISBN 0-7524-0028-2

Rhondda: A Second Selection
Simon Eckley and Emrys Jenkins
ISBN 0-7524-0308-7

Roath, Splott, and Adamsdown
Roath Local History Society
ISBN 0-7524-0199-8

GLOUCESTERSHIRE

Barnwood, Hucclecote and Brockworth
Alan Sutton
ISBN 0-7524-0000-2

Forest to Severn
Humphrey Phelps
ISBN 0-7524-0008-8

Filton and the Flying Machine
Malcolm Hall
ISBN 0-7524-0171-8

Gloster Aircraft Company
Derek James
ISBN 0-7524-0038-X

The City of Gloucester
Jill Voyce
ISBN 0-7524-0306-0

Around Nailsworth and Minchinhampton from the Conway Collection
Howard Beard
ISBN 0-7524-0048-7

Around Newent
Tim Ward
ISBN 0-7524-0003-7

Stroud: Five Stroud Photographers
Howard Beard, Peter Harris and Wilf Merrett
ISBN 0-7524-0305-2

HAMPSHIRE

Gosport
Ian Edelman
ISBN 0-7524-0300-1

Winchester from the Sollars Collection
John Brimfield
ISBN 0-7524-0173-4

HEREFORDSHIRE
Ross-on-Wye
Tom Rigby and Alan Sutton
ISBN 0-7524-0002-9

HERTFORDSHIRE
Buntingford
Philip Plumb
ISBN 0-7524-0170-X

Hampstead Garden Suburb
Mervyn Miller
ISBN 0-7524-0319-2

Hemel Hempstead
Eve Davis
ISBN 0-7524-0167-X

Letchworth
Mervyn Miller
ISBN 0-7524-0318-4

Welwyn Garden City
Angela Eserin
ISBN 0-7524-0133-5

KENT
Hythe
Joy Melville and Angela Lewis-Johnson
ISBN 0-7524-0169-6

North Thanet Coast
Alan Kay
ISBN 0-7524-0112-2

Shorts Aircraft
Mike Hooks
ISBN 0-7524-0193-9

LANCASHIRE
Lancaster and the Lune Valley
Robert Alston
ISBN 0-7524-0015-0

Morecambe Bay
Robert Alston
ISBN 0-7524-0163-7

Manchester
Peter Stewart
ISBN 0-7524-0103-3

LINCOLNSHIRE
Louth
David Cuppleditch
ISBN 0-7524-0172-6

Stamford
David Gerard
ISBN 0-7524-0309-5

LONDON
(Greater London and Middlesex)

Battersea and Clapham
Patrick Loobey
ISBN 0-7524-0010-X

Canning Town
Howard Bloch and Nick Harris
ISBN 0-7524-0057-6

Chiswick
Carolyn and Peter Hammond
ISBN 0-7524-0001-0

Forest Gate
Nick Harris and Dorcas Sanders
ISBN 0-7524-0049-5

Greenwich
Barbara Ludlow
ISBN 0-7524-0045-2

Highgate and Muswell Hill
Joan Schwitzer and Ken Gay
ISBN 0-7524-0119-X

Islington
Gavin Smith
ISBN 0-7524-0140-8

Lewisham
John Coulter and Barry Olley
ISBN 0-7524-0059-2

Leyton and Leytonstone
Keith Romig and Peter Lawrence
ISBN 0-7524-0158-0

Newham Dockland
Howard Bloch
ISBN 0-7524-0107-6

Norwood
Nicholas Reed
ISBN 0-7524-0147-5

Peckham and Nunhead
John D. Beasley
ISBN 0-7524-0122-X

Piccadilly Circus
David Oxford
ISBN 0-7524-0196-3

Around Leeds
Matthew Young and Dorothy Payne
ISBN 0-7524-0168-8

Penistone
Matthew Young and David Hambleton
ISBN 0-7524-0138-6

Selby from the William Rawling Collection
Matthew Young
ISBN 0-7524-0198-X

Central Sheffield
Martin Olive
ISBN 0-7524-0011-8

Around Stocksbridge
Stocksbridge and District History Society
ISBN 0-7524-0165-3

TRANSPORT

Filton and the Flying Machine
Malcolm Hall
ISBN 0-7524-0171-8

Gloster Aircraft Company
Derek James
ISBN 0-7524-0038-X

Great Western Swindon
Tim Bryan
ISBN 0-7524-0153-X

Midland and South Western Junction Railway
Mike Barnsley and Brian Bridgeman
ISBN 0-7524-0016-9

Shorts Aircraft
Mike Hooks
ISBN 0-7524-0193-9

This stock list shows all titles available in the United Kingdom as at 30 September 1995.

ORDER FORM

The books in this stock list are available from your local bookshop. Alternatively they are available by mail order at a totally inclusive price of £10.00 per copy.

For overseas orders please add the following postage supplement for each copy ordered:
> European Union £0.36 (this includes the Republic of Ireland)
> Royal Mail Zone 1 (for example, U.S.A. and Canada) £1.96
> Royal Mail Zone 2 (for example, Australia and New Zealand) £2.47

Please note that all of these supplements are actual Royal Mail charges with no profit element to the Chalford Publishing Company. Furthermore, as the Air Mail Printed Papers rate applies, we are restricted from enclosing any personal correspondence other than to indicate the senders name.

Payment can be made by cheque, Visa or Mastercard. Please indicate your method of payment on this order form.

If you are not entirely happy with your purchase you may return it within 30 days of receipt for a full refund.

Please send your order to:

> The Chalford Publishing Company,
> St Mary's Mill,
> Chalford,
> Stroud,
> Gloucestershire
> GL6 8NX

This order form should perforate away from the book. However, if you are reluctant to damage the book in any way we are quite happy to accept a photocopy order form or a letter containing the necessary information.

PLEASE WRITE CLEARLY USING BLOCK CAPITALS

Name and address of the person ordering the books listed below:

_____

_____

_____ Post code _____

Please also supply your telephone number in case we have difficulty fully understanding your requirements.   Tel.: _____ - _____

Name and address of where the books are to be despatched to (if different from above):

_____

_____

_____ Post code _____

Please indicate here if you would like to receive future information on books published by the Chalford Publishing Company.

_____ Yes, please put me on your mailing list   _____ No, please just send the books ordered below

Title	ISBN	Quantity
....	0-7524-_____-___	_____
....	0-7524-_____-___	_____
....	0-7524-_____-___	_____
....	0-7524-_____-___	_____
....	0-7524-_____-___	_____
	Total number of books	_____

Cost of books delivered in UK = Number of books ordered @ £10 each =£		_____
Overseas postage supplement (if relevant)	=£	_____
TOTAL PAYMENT	=£	_____

Method of Payment   ❑ Cheque   ❑ Visa   ❑ Mastercard   **VISA**

Please make cheques payable to *The Chalford Publishing Company*

MasterCard

Name of Card Holder   _____

Card Number ❑❑❑❑❑❑❑❑❑❑❑❑❑❑❑❑❑❑❑

Expiry date ❑❑ / ❑❑

I authorise payment of £_____ from the above card

Signed _____